FACET BOOKS

BIBLICAL SERIES

FACET fb BOOKS

BIBLICAL SERIES — 13

John Reumann, General Editor

The Problem of the Historical Jesus

by JOACHIM JEREMIAS

translated by Norman Perrin

FORTRESS PRESS PHILADELPHIA

An English version of this essay first appeared in *The Expository Times*, 69, 11 (August, 1958), pp. 333-39, under the title, "The Present Position in the Controversy concerning the Problem of the Historical Jesus." An expanded version appeared in the German series, "Calwer Hefte," edited by Theodor Schlatter, with the title *Das Problem des historischen Jesus* (No. 32; Stuttgart: Calwer Verlag, 1960, [5]1966). It was reprinted, again with minor changes, in the anthology edited by H. Ristow and K. Matthiae, *Der historische Jesus und der kerygmatische Christus* (Berlin: Evangelische Verlagsanstalt, 1962), pp. 12-25.

Library of Congress Catalog Card Number 64-23064

ISBN 0-8006-3015-7

Ninth printing 1980

8941J80 Printed in the United States of America 1-3015

Introduction

THE impressions which most of us have about Jesus of Nazareth change and develop over the years. For the first-grader in church school, Jesus is "our Friend and Helper." The same child, a few years later on, may have a fuller, more biographical picture of the Savior. For the high school or college student, critical problems arise, perhaps for the first time, about sources, or about Jesus' personality and aims, or about details in his life. If one begins to read the countless books on Jesus, or if one pursues further study in a seminary or university graduate school, serious questions may be posed about what Jesus did or did not say or do. Anyone who, over the course of the years, attempts to answer the question "What do you think of Christ?" will find that his answer is always, and increasingly, colored by his own experiences. What he thinks of Jesus is shaped and continually reshaped by his knowledge—or ignorance—of the original sources and by the way he uses them, or by the books he reads (whether those of William Barclay, or Paul Tillich, or Nikos Kazantzakis, or Alfred Edersheim). But a person's view of Jesus is also shaped by the age in which he happens to live, and by whether or not he agrees with the assumptions of his age, e.g., about the human situation or about the possibility of the miraculous. A man's opinion of the Nazarene may also be conditioned by the art at which he looks habitually—Sallman's "Head of Christ," a Dürer woodcut, a medieval Pietà, or the Rouault painting which adorns the cover of the Penguin edition of the *New English Bible* New Testament.

If all this marks the individual's experience in wrestling with the riddle of Jesus' life, then it should not surprise us that the experience of the church and of mankind as a whole is somewhat similar. Times change, and so do the outlooks of entire civilizations. We can scarcely expect that the answer about who Jesus was will be the same in medieval Rome and Reformation Wittenberg, in a pietist coventicle and in a rationalistic university like Tübingen at the beginning of the nineteenth century, or in Victorian England and Leninist Russia. And what do men think of Jesus now in a world "come of age"? It makes a profound difference whether one approaches this prophet who died upon a cross from the standpoint of medieval piety, or the Reformation principle of "grace alone," or the lordship of reason, or the nineteenth century's optimism about the world and man, or the twentieth century's more pessimistic existentialism. It also matters how much data we have that is relevant for understanding Jesus and his age (and here modern discoveries do put at our disposal more evidence on certain points than has been available at any time in almost two thousand years). But if our approach to this source material varies, and if our assumptions about methodology change from time to time, to say nothing of our presuppositions about God and the world, then it is not surprising to find that in the road of research into Jesus' life there have been many twists and turnings and some detours and dead ends. Just as in an individual's experience, so with *Leben-Jesu-Forschung*, as German scholarship terms the study of Jesus' life, there have been many new directions. In the last century of scholarly research, three stand out: an "Old Quest" of the historical Jesus; then, under new influences, a complete change in direction which led to the assumption that no biography is possible; and nowadays what is being spoken of as a "New Quest."

These three stages—the "Old Quest," the "no biography" point of view, and the "New Quest"—plus certain other influences have led to the current situation in the study of Jesus' life. The renewed interest in such research today, both on the highly technical level (where, for example, the type of Aramaic Jesus spoke is analyzed) and on the level of the average reader who wants to know the results of the scholars' toils, is heir of previous study, for better or for worse. Therefore, to comprehend the present situation and to be able to follow the controversies raging, some introduction is needed to show us how we have arrived where we are. One of the best guides, it is widely agreed, is the present essay by Professor Joachim Jeremias of Göttingen University. An English version of this lecture was first published in *The Expository Times* for August, 1958, under the title, "The Present Position in the Controversy concerning the Problem of the Historical Jesus." A later version, in which Professor Jeremias expanded several portions, usually by sharpening his remarks with regard to the discussion of the topic in Germany, was presented as a lecture in connection with the five-hundredth anniversary of Greifswald University in East Germany and then published in the series "Calwer Hefte" (1960). It was chosen by Helmut Ristow and Karl Matthiae to head the collection of essays compiled by them under the title *Der historische Jesus und der kerygmatische Christus* (1962). Even those who take a very different tack from Professor Jeremias in the New Quest recognize his presentation as a very useful summary of the past history and present situation in *Leben-Jesu-Forschung*. For almost any reader, the essay is a good starting-point for delving into one of the frontier areas in current biblical and theological study.

Professor Jeremias' credentials are excellent for guiding us into this debate in a lucid, judicious way. He was born into a family of Evangelical clergymen and scholars in Dresden in 1900. When he was a boy, he lived for some years in Jerusalem where his father, Friedrich Jeremias, was pastor at Redeemer

Lutheran Church. An uncle, Alfred Jeremias, was a famed Old Testament scholar. Thus from youth he acquired a first-hand acquaintance with the geography, languages, and customs of Palestine, a familiarity which he testifies has shed much new light on his understanding of biblical verses. From his mentor Gustav Dalman he learned even more about the ancient Palestinian sites and about Jesus' mother tongue–interests which have been reflected in his scholarly publications over the years. From 1929 to 1935 Dr. Jeremias was Professor of New Testament Studies at Greifswald; from 1935 till 1968 he held the chair in New Testament at Göttingen. Continuing the family tradition, his son Gert has now published his doctoral dissertation at Heidelberg, an important study on the Teacher of Righteousness at Qumran.

Though Professor Jeremias' professional interests have been widespread, they may be said to have centered in the historical Jesus. He has provided a number of significant monographs on aspects of the world and life and work of Jesus; many of them have already been translated into English. One of his books deals with the parables, and another with the "Words of Institution" spoken by Jesus in the Upper Room. In each case, with meticulous care, Professor Jeremias attempts to work back from the Greek accounts which the early church has given us in the gospels to the original Aramaic that Jesus spoke. Even those who disagree with Professor Jeremias' reconstructions on this point or that, grant that he has collected a wealth of material in each instance and has proceeded with an awareness of the difficulties involved. He himself knows the problems too well to assume that, at this distance, we can readily recover the "very words" *(ipsissima verba)* which Jesus spoke so long ago, but he does maintain that by exacting study we can hear again his "very voice" *(ipsissima vox)*. Compared with the endeavors of some scholars, those of Professor Jeremias here seem conservative and somewhat sanguine. Yet in the opinion of still other scholars he is quite unconservative when, in another book which examines sayings attributed to Jesus but preserved outside our canon, he concludes for the substantial authenticity of some of these "unknown sayings." In still other monographs on the background and use of the term "Servant of God" and on Jesus' attitude toward Gentiles, Professor Jeremias shows a similar interest in pressing back through the environment of that day to Jesus himself. Recent books in English include a volume of lectures given in the United States in 1963, a popular treatment of the parables, studies on the prayers of Jesus, and a detailed account of Jerusalem in Jesus' day. Current projects in retirement include a New Testament theology and a commentary, long under way, on the Gospel according to St. Luke.

In the current debate about the historical Jesus, Professor Jeremias' own position can best be assessed if we examine briefly the three great "swings of the pendulum" which have taken place in the last two centuries. Concern for what the man Jesus was really like is not, of course, a new thing. Apart from the much-debated question of how much biographical interest the evangelists themselves included among their intentions, it is a fact that the church fathers of the first few centuries, as well as their opponents, manifested just such an interest, as a recent book by Robert Grant has shown. The Middle Ages had their pictures of Jesus Christ, in dogma, drama, and in art. The Renaissance and Reformation, with their stress on historical studies, directed fresh attention to the man Jesus and to the biblical source materials. Protestant Orthodoxy had the effect, in its theology and writings, of harmonizing all the biblical accounts into one smooth composite—something which Tatian had already begun to do in the second century when he wove the four gospels into one account, the *Diatessaron*. A similar tendency to harmonize or conflate is also discernible in the history of liturgy where, for example, the "Words of Institution" recited at the Lord's Supper are usually a combination of the three gospel accounts and I Corinthians 11.

The first real change in the study of the life of Jesus, one which removed such study from the protective cover of

Christian piety, came with the rise of rationalism and critical Bible study in the eighteenth century. Professor Jeremias singles out the date of 1778 and the name of H. S. Reimarus (whose works were published posthumously by the German poet and man of letters, Lessing) for the start of what has come to be known as "the Quest of the Historical Jesus." Reimarus' age, the age of reason or "the Enlightenment," had begun to ask questions such as whether it is in John's Gospel or in the three Synoptics that we find preserved the most accurate picture of Jesus. Did he talk in parables (as the Synoptics portray him) or in long, allegorical discourses (as in John)? Did his ministry last one year (as the Synoptics suggest) or three (as John states)? Was the Temple cleansed on "Palm Sunday" (Matt. 21:10 ff.), "Palm Monday" (cf. Mark 11:12-19), or early in his ministry (John 2:13 ff.)? Or shall we rationalize and say he cleansed it twice (or thrice)? The upshot of all such questioning, and of Reimarus' even more probing work, was the assumption that a biography of Jesus "as he really was" could be reconstructed, in spite of the problems, if we could only learn how to evaluate our sources aright.

Hence there arose a search for the earliest and, it was assumed, most reliable sources about Jesus, and then, based on these, a Quest for the historical Jesus himself. This "Old Quest," as we now call it, resulted in innumerable "lives of Jesus." Though the movement has had its representatives down to our own day, it flowered especially between 1835 and 1900. Every German theologian of note had to write a *Leben Jesu*, and many a lesser light tried his hand too. Professor Jeremias briefly characterizes these ofttimes fantastic presentations, and interested readers can find fuller summaries in Albert Schweitzer's famous book *The Quest of the Historical Jesus*, or in subsequent survey articles. Some of these "lives" were real landmarks, like the "shocker" by D. F. Strauss in 1835-36, and some are still read today, like those of Ernest Renan, Geikie, or Stalker. Though these authors differed greatly in what they did with Jesus, their "lives" were usually dominated by the theology of the day, generally liberal in its tone, and always by the assumption that the historian could really recover Jesus accurately, in spite of later legend and dogma.

It is easy today to put one's finger on excesses and crippling weaknesses in the nineteenth-century Quest, but the movement also had its strengths which must be recognized. For one thing, these scholars of a century ago usually knew their sources in the original languages, and most of them had a proper concern for the historical figure of Jesus and a fear lest he dissolve into a vague spirit or "idea." Above all, they devoted themselves to the development of the historical method – that great nineteenth-century achievement which makes possible an approach to the Bible unattained in any previous century–and they worked toward a solution of the problem of the "sources" behind our written gospels. These elements–knowledge of the original documents, concern for the historical Jesus, and source criticism (as modified by subsequent investigation)–must be reckoned as abiding contributions of the nineteenth century to our position today.

But between 1900 and 1940 the pendulum swung again. Three factors emerged in this period which caused many scholars to reverse the optimistic hopes of the previous century and to conclude that, for scientific as well as for theological reasons, no biography of Jesus could ever be written. First came the rediscovery of eschatology. Nineteenth-century scholarship had come, by and large, to view Jesus as a great and noble teacher. His teachings about the fatherhood of God, the worth of the human soul, and the significance of love were hailed as Jesus' enduring insights. Any emphases in the gospels on "the End"–the whole area of eschatology and apocalyptic–were ignored or explained away as later accretions. Such were the views of scholars like William Wrede (1859-1906) and Adolf Harnack (1851-1930). But already in 1892 Johannes Weiss had published his little book *Die Predigt*

Jesu vom Reiche Gottes. His examination of the New Testament had driven him to the conclusion that Jesus' preaching was essentially eschatological and proclaimed the imminence of God's transcendental kingdom, but Weiss did not really know what to make of this observation and failed to apply it consistently. In 1906, however, Albert Schweitzer published his famous book *Von Reimarus zu Wrede* (as it was originally titled); it not only laid bare the failings of the nineteenth-century Quest, but it also proposed that eschatology was the key to the historical Jesus. According to Schweitzer, Jesus was obsessed with eschatology, a man aglow with expectations of the end of the world. Matthew 10:23 was a significant verse for Schweitzer, who regarded it as an authentic saying from a time when Jesus sent his twelve disciples forth to preach the imminence of the End: "You will not have gone through all the towns of Israel before the Son of man comes." But, alas, Jesus was wrong; the twelve made their preaching-tour of the towns of Israel, and no celestial figure put in his appearance on the clouds of heaven, bringing history to an end. After this delay in his eschatological program, Jesus, according to Schweitzer, had to readjust his thinking. He now decided that he must play an even greater eschatological role and go up to Jerusalem and, by his death, trigger the final eschatological explosion which would end world history with the revelation of the Son of man. Eagerly he embraced the cross—and died a disappointed eschatologist, noble but mistaken. Even his ethical teachings have no abiding significance, for they were intended just for the interim, that brief moment of heroic living before the world went under.

Orthodox theology, both Protestant and Catholic, faced a real dilemma here. If Wrede and others like him were right, Jesus was a non-eschatological teacher of morality. If Schweitzer's views were correct, then Jesus was something different from the mere ethical teacher: he was an apocalyptist, but one who had been completely wrong! Of course, more recent New Testament studies scarcely read the evidence this way, as if "eschatology" and "ethics" were an "either/or," and Professor Jeremias lays stress on a programmatic book by Martin Kähler in 1892 which was to point in a totally new direction from the disputes occasioned by the nineteenth-century Quest and even by Schweitzer's work. But the fact remains that Albert Schweitzer introduced an element into *Leben-Jesu-Forschung* which had for the most part been previously overlooked. Failure to wrestle with the eschatological question vitiated most of the earlier "lives." Since Schweitzer's day the eschatological element cannot be ignored.

The second factor which changed the terrain of New Testament studies was the emergence of form criticism after the First World War. Form criticism is the attempt to see what happened to the stories about Jesus and sayings attributed to him during the period when they were circulated solely by word of mouth, in the period between A.D. 30 and 50 or 80. The form critical method had originally been developed in Old Testament studies and was now applied in a fruitful way to the New Testament by a trio of German scholars, Rudolf Bultmann, Martin Dibelius, and K. L. Schmidt. While Professor Jeremias has not been particularly identified with this phase of New Testament studies, he accepts form criticism as a recognized and valuable tool, especially for working back behind the Greek accretions in our gospels to the Palestinian, Aramaic level. The methodological problem, as Professor Jeremias notes, is that once we recover something "Palestinian," we cannot be immediately certain whether this comes from Jesus himself or from the Aramaic-speaking church in Palestine. Jesus was not the only person in the first century to speak Aramaic! Many leading exponents of form criticism, like Bultmann, tend to lay far more emphasis on the early church than on Jesus. In their view, form criticism helps us penetrate back to what the primitive community believed on this point or that, but we cannot be positive that this was Jesus' own opinion. Hence, form criticism, by stressing the role of the early church in transmitting, shaping, and even creating the material about Jesus, serves, in this view, to make us more dubious about getting back behind the post-resurrection community to the historical Jesus.

A third factor accounting for the view that no biography of Jesus is really possible is the changed understanding of history that began to grow up among certain philosophers and historians. For a long time it had been assumed (as it perhaps still is by a majority of people) that historical facts exist quite independently and objectively, and that the job of the scientific historian is to recover them from the sources. In this view, the study of history is an "I-it" relationship: history is an "it" which I, the objective scholar, observe and recover. In this view the historian is an impartial spectator. A more recent view of history, however, prefers to think in different terms: the study of history is an "I-thou" relation; the scholar does not preside over his study with lordly detachment, for even if he is centuries removed from his subject, he still has existential questions, arising out of his own existence as a human being, and he is aware of his own presuppositions and has no allusions about what he can prove historically. This changed view of history is represented in the English-speaking world notably by the late R. G. Collingwood of Oxford, or E. H. Carr of Cambridge. It has affinities with some of the distinctions made by Martin Kähler with regard to study of the gospels, which Professor Jeremias points out. It may be reflected in the despair about history found in Karl Barth, or in the position that Søren Kierkegaard was voicing during the century of the Old Quest. Utterly unconcerned with the "scientific" reconstructions of modern scholars, Kierkegaard once wrote, "If the contemporary generation [of Jesus] had left nothing behind them but these words: 'We have believed that in such and such a year the God appeared among us in the humble form of a servant, that he lived and taught in our community, and finally died,' it would be more than enough" *(Philosophical Fragments* [Princeton University Press, [2]1962], p. 130).

The New Testament scholar who has taken up this position in a thorough-going way and applied it to the life of Jesus is Rudolf Bultmann, who though now retired from his position as Professor of New Testament at Marburg (1921-51) continues to exercise a great influence through his writings and through the pupils whom he has trained. In his critical examination of the sources about Jesus, Bultmann found little of historical reliability, but he seemed to revel in this hopelessness. He put his emphasis instead on what he did find in the New Testament: the kerygma, or proclamation of the early church about the exalted Christ. For Bultmann, all the old "life of Jesus" fantasies can "burn," they have no value for faith. It is not the "Christ after the flesh" that matters, not Christ "from a human point of view" (II Cor. 5:16), but only the risen, exalted Lord who confronts men (historians included) in the proclamation of the word. Hence Bultmann finds little to say, historically or theologically, about Jesus; his is a "theology of the kerygma."

These three factors, then, help to account for what must be called the prevailing view, at least in German theological circles, until about 1953. This view rejected, on scientific and theological grounds, the possibility and even the desirability of a life of Jesus and exulted in this situation, seeing in it a defense of what "faith" really must mean. Professor Jeremias finds both strengths and dangers in such a position.

Finally the pendulum has swung a third time, not back to the extremes of the nineteenth-century Quest, but at least away from the "no biography" extreme, back toward the center and toward some interest in the Jesus of history. Oddly enough, while there have always been some scholars (including Professor Jeremias himself) who have declined to agree with the position of the Bultmann school, the real reaction, leading to a "New Quest," came from among Professor Bultmann's own pupils. At a gathering of former Marburg students in 1953, Professor Ernst Käsemann read a now-famous paper proposing such a quest which, avoiding the errors of the nineteenth-century fiasco, would attempt to say something more of the Jesus behind the kerygma than Bultmann had. What dogmaticians like Paul Althaus had been calling for, Bultmannians like Käsemann and Ernst Fuchs now began to take up as historically possible and theologically legitimate. Professor Jeremias refers at points in this essay to some of their work. The hopes and procedures of the New Quest have been described in a number of places, notably in a book by James M. Robinson, and the "first fruits," as it were, was a paperback (soon translated into English) by Günther Bornkamm, *Jesus von Nazareth.* While the New Quest continues to recognize the kerygma as the "cutting-edge" of the gospel (always viewing Jesus as the Christ, and never just as Jesus), and while a "proved" Jesus Christ is still regarded as both historically impossible and theologically a contradiction, it is held that a quest back through the kerygma will reveal a Jesus behind it who, particularly in his sayings, is consistent with, and of a pattern with, the church's proclamation.

It is this current New Quest which provides the immediate background for Professor Jeremias' essay. No more can be said about the subject here, except to indicate that countless articles and books have appeared in the past five years about the controversy to which we are here so ably introduced. Two large anthology volumes in German, several collections of essays in English, plus articles in journals, a survey by R. H. Fuller, an excellent account by the German journalist and theologian Heinz Zahrnt, and a more detailed analysis by Hugh Anderson can be consulted for a more complete picture.

If readers want to sample lives of Jesus for themselves, they can of course find any number of the nineteenth-century efforts, written from varying perspectives, still available (e.g., Renan, Keim, Edersheim), or their more recent counterparts (Bruce Barton, Giovanni Papini, Sholem Asch, Kagawa, Fulton Oursler, or Jim Bishop). Bultmann's *Jesus* is available in paperback. Bornkamm's *Jesus of Nazareth* offers difficult but rewarding reading. Three recent lives by Morton S. Enslin, Ethelbert Stauffer, and S. Vernon McCasland, are harder to classify, but reflect more of the Old Quest than of either kerygma-theology or the New Quest. Enslin represents the liberal tradition; there is little use of form criticism, but the pungent style and challenging judgments are meant to help the reader see vividly the sort of man Jesus was: one whom his contemporaries did understand—and crucified. Stauffer claims to employ "new sources" and often reflects quite conservative positions; but his tendency is to pit Jesus against Paul (and the kerygma), and this would mark his work as basically Old Quest rather than New. McCasland does not want to give us only biography (for which he feels we have some source materials); he also desires to enter into the mind and faith of Jesus himself, and exhibits psychological interest in Jesus' encounters with God. To cite one other recent example: a book illustrating how a scholar with interests in systematic theology and with awareness of current New Testament studies approaches the life of Jesus in a positive way is *The Day of His Coming* by Gerhard Gloege. Perhaps Gloege's book is the best one to begin with, if one wishes to see how one can write meaningfully of Jesus, in a theological perspective, for all the current debate.

As to Professor Jeremias' own position in this discussion, it is clear that he is not part of the Old Quest, for he is quite aware of its failures. He is likewise not an enthusiast for "kerygma-theology," for he is concerned to separate the gospel of Jesus from the kerygma of the early church. I should not even classify him as part of the "New Questors," for Professor Jeremias never abandoned the task or gave up hope the way the Bultmann school did. I should call his position that of "discerning continuity" with what is worthwhile in past research. This sort of continuity he may be said to share with scholars like Maurice Goguel in France and T. W. Manson in England, among others. Goguel published his *Vie de Jésus* in 1932, just a few years after Bultmann's *Jesus*. He was aware of the failures of the Old Quest, he knew and used form criticism, but he also preserved an interest in the Jesus of history. His book was translated into English the next year, but Anglo-Saxon readers, unaware of developments in continental scholarship and accustomed to the sort of "life" presented by T. R. Glover and his generation, did not know what to make of a book that spent two hundred pages on prolegomena and produced such negative results on so many issues. Manson, who also operated with the tools of modern critical scholarship and with an awareness of nineteenth-century shortcomings, viewed the task as "The Quest of the Historical Jesus–Continued," as he entitled a lecture delivered four years before Käsemann galvanized the Marburgers into a New Quest. In many ways, Professor Jeremias fits into the company of those who think of the quest as "continued," and his present essay describes the "why" and "how" for a continuing quest.

The original translation into English for *The Expository Times* in 1958 was done by Norman Perrin, now of the Divinity School of the University of Chicago. The additions in the subsequent versions published in German have been inserted and a number of changes in phraseology made, with the approval of Professor Jeremias, by the Editor, who has also revised and expanded the notes for the American edition.

Some readers may be surprised to find, as Professor Jeremias unfolds the topic, that study of the Jesus of history involves us in questions not only about the historical method but also about our understanding of revelation, ourselves, and our concept of God. Such a discovery would not surprise the authors of the gospels. One of them wrote, as he looked back at his attempt to interpret the world of things which Jesus did, "These things have been recorded that you may come to believe and hold the faith that Jesus is the Messiah, God's Son, and that, believing, you may possess life through his name" (John 20:31). Such an understanding of what telling the story of Jesus involves, immediately implies far more than straight reporting.

JOHN REUMANN

Lutheran Theological Seminary
Philadelphia
April, 1967

Contents

THE PROBLEM OF THE HISTORICAL JESUS

To anyone who is not aware of the controversy,[1] the question whether the historical Jesus and his message have any significance for the Christian faith must sound absurd. No one in the ancient church, no one in the church of the Reformation period and of the two succeeding centuries thought of asking such a question. How is it possible that today this question is being asked in all seriousness, that it even occupies a central place in New Testament debate, and that in many quarters

[1] Among the more pertinent books and articles in the extensive literature on the subject are the following: Martin Kähler, *Der sogenannte historische Jesus und der geschichtliche, biblische Christus* (Leipzig: A. Deichertsche Verlagsbuchhandlung, 1892; [2]1896; new ed., ed. E. Wolf ["Theologische Bücherei," 2; Munich: Kaiser, 1953]); Eng. trans. by Carl E. Braaten, *The So-called Historical Jesus and the Historic, Biblical Christ* (Philadelphia: Fortress Press, 1964). Albert Schweitzer, *Geschichte der Leben-Jesu-Forschung* (Tübingen: J. C. B. Mohr, 1906; [2]1913; [6]1951); Eng. trans. by W. Montgomery, *The Quest of the Historical Jesus: A Critical Study of its Progress from Reimarus to Wrede* (London: A. & C. Black, 1910; [2]1911). Rudolf Bultmann, *Theologie des Neuen Testaments* (Tübingen: J. C. B. Mohr, 1948-53; [5]1965); Eng. trans. by Kendrick Grobel, *Theology of the New Testament,* (2 vols.; New York: Scribner's, 1951-55). Ernst Käsemann, "Das Problem des historischen Jesus," *Zeitschrift für Theologie und Kirche,* 51 (1954), 125-53; Eng. trans. by W. J. Montague, *Essays on New Testament Themes* ("Studies in Biblical Theology," No. 41; London: SCM, 1964), pp. 15-47. Nils A. Dahl, "Der historische Jesus als geschichtswissenschaftliches und theologisches Problem," *Kerygma und Dogma,* 1 (1955), 104-32; Eng. trans., "The Problem of the Historical Jesus," in *Kerygma and History: A Symposium on the Theology of Rudolf Bultmann,* ed. Carl E. Braaten and Roy A. Harrisville (New York: Abingdon, 1962), pp. 138-71. T. W. Manson, "The life of Jesus: some tendencies in present-day research," in *The Background of the New Testament and its Eschatology* (in honour of Charles Harold Dodd), ed. W. D.

it is being answered with a decisive negative? For a widely held theological position maintains that the historical Jesus and his message have no, or at least no decisive, significance for the Christian faith. We ask: (1) Why is such a point of view possible? How has it arisen? What is its basis? (2) What can be said by way of criticism of this view? and (3) What is the relation between the good tidings of Jesus and the proclamation of the church?

Davies and D. Daube (Cambridge University Press, 1956), pp. 211-21. Ernst Heitsch, "Die Aporie des historischen Jesus als Problem theologischer Hermeneutik," *Zeitschrift für Theologie und Kirche,* 53 (1956), 192-210. Ernst Fuchs, "Die Frage nach dem historischen Jesus," *Zeitschrift für Theologie und Kirche,* 53, (1956), 210-29; Eng. trans. by A. Scobie, "The Quest of the Historical Jesus," in *Studies of the Historical Jesus* ("Studies in Biblical Theology," 42; London: SCM, 1964), pp. 11-31. Joachim Jeremias, *Die Gleichnisse Jesu* (Zurich: Zwingli-Verlag, 1947; Göttingen: Vandenhoeck & Ruprecht, [7]1965); Eng. trans. by S. H. Hooke, *The Parables of Jesus* (London: SCM, and New York: Scribner's, 1954; rev. ed., 1963). Béda Rigaux, "Jésus-Christ devant l'histoire et la dialectique," *Revue Générale Belge,* 94 (1958-59), pp. 1-16. Paul Althaus, *Das sogenannte Kerygma und der historische Jesus: Zur Kritik der heutigen Kerygma-Theologie* ("Beiträge zur Förderung christlicher Theologie," 48; Gütersloh: Bertelsmann, 1958); Eng. trans. by David Cairns, *The So-Called Kerygma and the Historical Jesus* (Edinburgh: Oliver and Boyd, 1959); in its U.S. edition, *Fact and Faith in the Kerygma of Today* (Philadelphia: Muhlenberg, 1960). James M. Robinson, *A New Quest of the Historical Jesus* ("Studies in Biblical Theology," 25; London: SCM, and Naperville: Allenson, 1959); German trans., *Kerygma und historischer Jesus* (Zurich: Zwingli-Verlag, 1960). Rudolf Schnackenburg, "Jesusforschung und Christusglaube," *Catholica,* 13 (1959), 1-17. *Die Frage nach dem historischen Jesus, Zeitschrift für Theologie und Kirche,* 56 (1959), Beiheft, 1, with contributions from Hans Conzelmann, Gerhard Ebeling, and Ernst Fuchs; Eng. trans. of Conzelmann's paper, "The Method of the Life-of-Jesus Research," in *The Historical Jesus and the Kerygmatic Christ: Essays on the New Quest of the Historical Jesus,* ed. Carl E. Braaten and Roy A. Harrisville (New York: Abingdon, 1964), pp. 54-68; Eng. trans. by J. W. Leitch of Ebeling's paper, "The Question of the Historical Jesus and the Problem of Christology," in *Word and Faith* (Philadelphia: Fortress Press, 1963), pp. 288-304. Rudolf Bultmann, *Das Verhältnis der urchristlichen Christusbotschaft zum historischen Jesus* (Sitzungsberichte der Heidelberger Akademie der Wissenschaften, philosoph.-hist. Klasse, 1960:3; third ed., Heidelberg: Carl Winter Universitätsverlag, 1962); Eng. trans. in *The Historical Jesus and the Kerygmatic Christ, op. cit.,* pp. 15-42; much of what has been written in the controversy in the last decade (mostly in German) may be gathered from this essay and its notes. The American reader may especially consult James M. Robinson, *A New Quest, op. cit.,* and Reginald H. Fuller, *The New Testament in Current Study* (New York: Scribner's, 1962); both authors are, on the whole, favorable to the Bultmannian outlook but try to reach a position of their own beyond him.

1

THE THEOLOGY OF THE KERYGMA

IN order to understand the "theology of the kerygma,"[2] as represented by Rudolf Bultmann and his school, it is necessary to retrace the route by which this position has been reached. We shall here attempt to sketch that route in broad outline.

HERMANN SAMUEL REIMARUS

The problem of the historical Jesus is of recent origin; the date of its birth can be precisely fixed at 1778. That date tells us that the problem of the historical Jesus is a child of the Enlightenment. Previous centuries held fast to the position that the gospels give us absolutely reliable information about Jesus; they saw no problem here. New Testament study of the gospels in the two centuries before the Enlightenment essentially confined itself to the task of paraphrasing and harmonizing the four gospels. In practice New Testament exegesis was a handmaid to the study of dogmatics. It was at the end of the eighteenth century that it was first recognized that the historical Jesus and the Christ proclaimed in the gospels and by the church are not the same. The man who announced this with

2 ["Kerygma" represents a Greek term meaning "proclamation," found eight times in the New Testament. It is used to denote the early Christian proclamation that Jesus Christ is lord, and refers both to the content of that proclamation and to the action of preaching it; cf. I Cor. 1:21; Rom. 16:25; or Titus 1:3, for examples. The primacy of the kerygma in New Testament studies and its centrality for all theology have been stressed especially by Bultmann and his pupils.—EDITOR.]

brutal candor was Hermann Samuel Reimarus. Born in Hamburg in 1694, he was a professor of oriental languages, i.e., he was not a theologian. He died in 1768 in his native city. At his death he left a manuscript which came into the hands of Gotthold Ephraim Lessing, who, between 1774 and 1778, published seven excerpts from it. The seventh piece bore the title *Von dem Zwecke Jesu und seiner Jünger: Noch ein Fragment des Wolfenbüttelschen Ungenannten.*[3] We must, says Reimarus, distinguish between the "aim" of Jesus, that is, the purpose which he set before himself, and the "aim" of his disciples. Jesus' purpose must be understood in the light of the cry from the cross, "My God, my God, why hast thou forsaken me?"–words which proclaimed the failure of his purpose. That is to say: Jesus was a Jewish political Messiah, who sought to set up an earthly kingdom and to deliver the Jews from a foreign yoke. His cry from the cross shows that his "aim" had not been achieved. The "aim" of his disciples was totally different. Confronted by the collapse of their dreams, what were they to do? They had no wish to return to their trade. But how were they to live? They contrived to steal the corpse of Jesus and, by inventing the message of his resurrection and return, gathered adherents. Hence it was the disciples who created the figure of Christ.

Great agitation followed upon the publication of this hate-filled pamphlet, and it rightly met with general rejection. Hate is no guide to historical truth. Nevertheless, Reimarus, the outsider, had been the first to perceive clearly a fact which had hitherto been overlooked. He had seen that the Jesus of history and the Christ preached by the church are not the same. History and dogma are two different things. The problem of the historical Jesus starts with Reimarus. Albert

[3] ["Concerning the Aim of Jesus and his Disciples: Another Fragment by the Anonymous Author from Wolfenbüttel"], Braunschweig, 1778. [For a partial translation, cf. *Fragments from Reimarus consisting of Brief Critical Remarks on the Object of Jesus and his Disciples . . .* , edited by Charles Voysey (London: Williams and Norgate, 1879; reprinted, Lexington, Kentucky: American Theological Seminary Library Association, 1962).—EDITOR.]

Schweitzer rightly entitled the first edition of his history of the study of the life of Jesus *Von Reimarus zu Wrede*.[4]

Reimarus to Kähler

Reimarus' portrayal of the historical Jesus was clearly absurd and amateurish. Jesus was no political revolutionary. Our sources bear unambiguous and trustworthy testimony to the fact that he was sharply opposed to the nationalistic Zealot tendencies in the world of his day. Still, in his contention that the historical Jesus was different from the Christ as depicted in the gospels, notably in John, Reimarus had raised a question which could not be evaded, namely, who really was Jesus of Nazareth?

The study of the life of Jesus in which the Enlightenment now engaged sought to answer precisely this question. This study was inspired by a liberal theology and, indeed, represented a revolt against ecclesiastical dogma. This whole scholarly activity, centered on the historical Jesus, represented an attempt to break loose from dogma. The battle cry was, "Back to Jesus, the man from Nazareth!" Not christological dogma, but the personality and religion of Jesus were the decisive factors.

Under the aegis of this watchword a multitude of lives of Jesus came into being, and we smile as we read them today. These lives vary greatly. The rationalists pictured Jesus as a preacher of morality, the idealists as the ideal Man; the aesthetes extolled him as the master of words and the socialists as the friend of the poor and as the social reformer, while the innumerable pseudo-scholars made of him a fictional character.[5] Jesus was modernized. These lives of Jesus are mere products of wishful thinking. The final outcome was that every epoch and every theology found in the personality of Jesus the reflection of its own ideals, and every author the reflection

[4] Tübingen, 1906; for Eng. trans., see note 1.

[5] Cf. J. Leipoldt, *Vom Jesusbilde der Gegenwart* (Leipzig: Dörffling & Franke, 1913; [2]1925).

of his own views. What had gone wrong? It was that, unconsciously, dogma had been replaced by psychology and fantasy. For all these lives of Jesus have one thing in common: their delineation of the personality of Jesus had been achieved by means of these two things, psychology and fantasy. The main share of the responsibility rests, not with the sources alone, but with the modern writers' uncontrolled psychologizing. It was a real tragedy that Albert Schweitzer, who throughout his whole book had exposed with ruthless insight the true nature of this wishful thinking, should himself have been ensnared by the fallacy of psychological reconstruction when he interpreted Matthew 10:23 to mean that Jesus' disappointment concerning his expectations of the imminent parousia brought the great turning point in his life, leading him to embark upon the way of the cross as the means to force the coming of God's kingdom.

At first the so-called positive theology[6] wisely confined itself essentially to warding off these attempts at reconstruction, and hence to an apologetic stance. Not until 1892 did positive theology pass over to the attack with a programmatic book by Martin Kähler, a book in advance of its time and embodying a specific thesis: *Der sogenannte historische Jesus und der geschichtliche, biblische Christus.*[7] The title of this work must

[6] [As employed in nineteenth-century biblical studies in Germany, "positive theology" designated the position of those who, while wishing, in varying degrees, to employ the tools of historical scholarship, rejected the "negative" and often theologically liberal conclusions of many of the critical scholars. In life-of-Jesus research it opposed a "life" like that by Ernest Renan.–EDITOR.]

[7] [*The So-called Historical Jesus and the Historic, Biblical Christ, op. cit.* To make a distinction in English between *historisch* and *geschichtlich* is the despair of most translators. Reginald Fuller, followed by many others, has adopted "historical" or "past-historical" for the former, and "historic" for the latter, in his rendering of essays in *Kerygma and Myth,* Vol. 1, ed. H. W. Bartsch (London: SPCK, and Greenwich: Seabury, 1953), pp. xi-xii. Some challenge the distinction made even in German and feel that it is quite arbitrary in English. Cf., however, *Webster's Third New International Dictionary* (Springfield, Mass.: G. & C. Merriam, 1961), p. 1073; "historical" is defined as ". . . having the character of history," and "historic" as "having . . . significance, or consequence." Professor Jeremias' explanation clarifies well what Kähler meant.—EDITOR.]

be carefully examined if we wish to understand Kähler's thesis. Kähler distinguishes, on the one hand, between "Jesus" and "Christ," and, on the other hand, between *historisch* ("historical") and *geschichtlich* ("historic"). "Jesus" denoted for Kähler the man of Nazareth, as the lives of Jesus had described and were describing him, while "Christ" denoted the Savior proclaimed by the church. The term *historisch* meant for him the bare facts of the past, while *geschichtlich* meant that which possesses abiding significance. That is, he placed over against one another the so-called "historical Jesus," as the writers of the lives of Jesus had sought to reconstruct him, and the "historic, biblical Christ," as the apostles had proclaimed him. His thesis runs: only the biblical Christ can be apprehended by us, and he alone is of abiding significance for faith. Only as the gospels portray him for us, and not as the self-styled scientific reconstructions present him, does "the undeniable impression of the fullest reality" make its impact upon us.[8] It should be noted—because it is often overlooked—that Kähler was convinced of the "reliability" of the "vivid and coherent image of a Man, an image we never fail to recognize," that confronts us in the New Testament records.[9] At first, however, Kähler's challenge went unheard; only in our time, when Rudolf Bultmann took it up and reformulated it, has it come into its own.

Modern Critical Theology

Inaugurated by Rudolf Bultmann and under his influence a truly fascinating development has taken place in recent decades. After a hundred and fifty years of preoccupation with the historical Jesus, critical theology came to recognize that it had undertaken an impossible task; it had the courage to acknowledge this fact openly, and with banners flying went over into the enemy camp. It turned its back on its history, it endorsed Kähler's views, at least in their negative aspects, it

[8] Kähler, *The So-called Historical Jesus*, p. 78.

[9] *Ibid.*, pp. 89, 95.

declared its preoccupation with the historical Jesus to have been an insoluble and fruitless undertaking, and it withdrew into the invulnerable bastion of the kerygma, the proclamation about Christ.

Critical theology has based its renunciation of the historical Jesus and return to the apostolic preaching about Christ upon two considerations.

(1) It points to the peculiar character of our sources. We have no writings from the hand of Jesus, such as we possess from the hand of the apostle Paul. On the contrary, we know Jesus only from the gospels, which are not biographies but testimonies of faith. The gospels contain a great deal of material which has been extensively edited in the course of transmission, and many legends (one need refer only to the miracle stories). All four gospels picture Jesus as he is apprehended by the faith of the evangelists: Mark depicts the hidden Son of God; Matthew, the secret King of Israel; Luke, the Lord of the future church; John, the self-revealing Son of God. From this material, as a hundred unavailing attempts have shown, it is not possible to construct a life of Jesus. We must free ourselves from the subjectivity of the so-called "historical Jesus research." We must draw the full consequences of the fact that we can know Jesus only as clad in the garb of myth. We must acknowledge that we cannot go behind the kerygma; if we attempt to do so nonetheless, we shall find ourselves on shaky ground.

(2) Now it is not as if the sources left us entirely in the lurch, says critical theology. The time is past when an unscientific skepticism could doubt whether Jesus had ever lived at all. On the contrary, we can gain considerable information about Jesus himself and also about his proclamation. But what we arrive at when we analyze the sources with the tools of historical research, says critical theology, yields nothing that would be of significance for faith. For this Jesus of Nazareth was a Jewish prophet. To be sure, he was a prophet who, since he demanded absolute obedience, saw mankind as totally sinful,

and proclaimed divine forgiveness to men, had apprehended "the Jewish conception of God in its purity and consistency."[10] He was indeed a prophet who claimed that a man's attitude toward His word determined his attitude toward God. But, for all that, he remained within the framework of Judaism. What he preached was a more radicalized form of Old Testament, Jewish faith in God.[11] For Bultmann, the history of Jesus is part of the history of Judaism, not of Christianity. To be sure, this Jewish prophet is of historical interest for New Testament theology, but he neither has, nor can have, significance for Christian faith, since (and here we have an astonishing thesis) Christianity first began at Easter. Here a decisive point has been reached. Who would ever think of saying that Islam began after Mohammed's death, or Buddhism after the death of Buddha? If we accept the thesis that Christianity began at Easter with the proclamation about the risen Christ, then indeed the logical inference is that, since Jesus was only a Jewish prophet, he does not belong to Christianity. "The message of Jesus," so runs the opening sentence of Bultmann's *Theology of the New Testament*, "belongs to the presuppositions of the theology of the New Testament and is not a part of that theology itself."[12] Here the plural, "presuppositions," must be especially noted. It implies that the message of Jesus is one presupposition of New Testament theology among many others, and perhaps not even the decisive one. Other factors are just as important: the Easter experiences of the disciples, the messianic expectations of Judaism, and the mythology of the pagan world which provided the garment with which Jesus of Nazareth was to be

[10] R. Bultmann, *Jesus* ("Die Unsterblichen," 1; Berlin: Deutsche Bibliothek, 1926), p. 143. Eng. trans. by Louise Pettibone Smith and Erminie Huntress, *Jesus and The Word* (New York: Scribner's, 1934), p. 155.

[11] R. Bultmann, *Theologie des Neuen Testaments, op. cit.*, p. 12; in the Eng. trans., *op. cit.*, cf. Vol. 1, pp. 3 ff., especially 4, 12, 16-17, and 22-26.

[12] *Op. cit.* [In the Eng. trans., see Vol. 1, p. 3, where the rendering, "*The message of Jesus* is a presupposition . . .," does not quite bring out the full sense of ". . . gehört zu den Voraussetzungen . . ." or make quite the point to which Professor Jeremias refers above.—EDITOR.]

clothed. The study of Jesus and his message may be very interesting and instructive for the historical understanding of the rise of Christianity, but it has no significance for faith.

These, then, are the two bases upon which modern critical theology rests its rejection of the historical Jesus. (1) We cannot write a life of Jesus because the requisite sources are lacking, and (2) what we can regard as historical is a Jewish prophet and his message, neither of which has any significance for faith. Hence it follows that our task today is not to pursue the phantom of the historical Jesus, but to interpret the kerygma, that is, the message of the apostle Paul about the justification of sinners. Admittedly, the Christianity of the Pauline and Johannine communities is a specimen of the syncretism of the Hellenistic period, and as such reflects the religious climate of that day.[13] But this is not an insuperable difficulty. We must demythologize the message and translate it into modern terms, with, let us say, the help of existentialist philosophy.

Gerhard Ebeling states these ideas very bluntly when he says that revelation is not "a historical datum" (*ein historisches Faktum*),[14] nor is it "a historic event" (*ein geschichtliches Geschehen*).[15] Revelations was not accomplished and completed during the years 1-30. Rather, it continues to take place whenever the kerygma is preached; it takes place in the act of faith.[16]

In surveying this position we have outlined, we must first point out its positive aspects. Today critical research is very different from what it was in the previous century. It is bent

[13] R. Bultmann, *Das Urchristentum im Rahmen der antiken Religionen* (Zurich: Artemis-Verlag, 1949; [2]1954); Eng. trans. by R. H. Fuller, *Primitive Christianity in its Contemporary Setting* ("Living Age Books"; New York: Meridian, 1956).

[14] *Die Geschichtlichkeit der Kirche und ihre Verkündigung als theologisches Problem* (Tübingen: J. C. B. Mohr, 1954), p. 59; Eng. trans. by Grover Foley, *The Problem of Historicity in the Church and its Proclamation* (Philadelphia: Fortress Press, 1967), p. 72.

[15] *Ibid.,* pp. 59 ff; Eng. trans., p. 73.

[16] *Ibid.,* p. 63; Eng. trans., p. 77.

on taking the entire kerygma into account and giving it its full due. The positive significance of this new stance of critical theology is of course immense. Nevertheless, I can see very grave dangers in this position. They are these: we are in danger of surrendering the affirmation "the Word became flesh" and of dissolving "salvation history," God's activity in the man Jesus of Nazareth and in his message; we are in danger of Docetism,[17] where Christ becomes an idea; we are in danger of putting the proclamation of the apostle Paul in the place of the good tidings of Jesus.

17 ["Docetism," from the Greek *dokéin,* to "appear" or "seem," refers to those types of Christian teaching where God is held to have become not really incarnate but only to have "appeared" to become man. It thus undervalues the reality of the life of Jesus.—EDITOR.]

2

THE CRUCIAL SIGNIFICANCE OF THE HISTORICAL JESUS

WHAT can be said by way of criticism of the position which we have outlined?

THE NECESSITY OF HISTORICAL STUDY

(1) Without a doubt it is true to say that the dream of ever writing a biography of Jesus is over. It would be disastrous if we were unwilling to heed critical scholarship's salutary caution regarding uncritical use of the gospels. Nevertheless we *must* go back to the historical Jesus and his message. We cannot bypass him. Quite apart from all theological considerations, there are two circumstances which compel us to make the attempt to ascertain the character of the gospel as Jesus proclaimed it. First of all, it is *the sources* which forbid us to confine ourselves to the kerygma of the primitive church and which force us ever and again to raise the question of the historical Jesus and his message. Every verse of the gospels tells us that the origin of Christianity lies not in the kerygma, not in the resurrection experiences of the disciples, not in a "Christ-idea." Every verse tells us, rather, that the origin of Christianity lies in the appearance of the man who was crucified under Pontius Pilate, Jesus of Nazareth, and in his message. I must emphasize the last words—*and his message*. The gospel that Jesus proclaimed antedates the kerygma of the primitive community. And as uncertain as many a detail of Jesus' life

may be, his message can be clearly ascertained. To be sure, the accounts of Jesus and his message were recounted by the early church as testimonies to its faith, and the gospels are, to be sure, not biographies in the sense of the Greek biographies (that much we have learned). Nevertheless there has been gross exaggeration here. It is not as though everything in the gospels is colored and shaped by the faith of the church and the evangelists. Paul wrote earlier than all four evangelists, and he was *the* great theologian in the Gentile Christian church before the composition of the gospels. But Pauline terminology is discernible only here and there in the gospels. Jesus cannot be relegated to the rank and file of an anonymous primitive community. Over and over again we come across words which unmistakably imply a situation prior to Easter. Only occasionally do we meet with traces here and there of christological overlay; and even if everything were overlaid with Christology, the study of the historical Jesus would still remain an imperative task, since the absence of primary sources should not constitute a reason for abandoning historical research.

(2) But it is not only the sources which compel us to keep on raising the problem of the historical Jesus and his message; the kerygma, too, the preaching about Christ by the early church, leads us back from itself at every turn. For the kerygma refers to a historical event. It proclaims: God was in Christ and reconciled the world to himself. God revealed himself in an event in history. The very heart of the kerygma, that "Christ died for our sins in accordance with the scriptures" (I Corinthians 15:3), represents an interpretation of a historical event: this death happened for us. But this raises the question whether this interpretation of the crucifixion of Jesus has been arbitrarily impressed upon the events, or whether there was some circumstance in the events which caused this interpretation to be attached to it. In other words, we must ask: Did Jesus himself speak of his impending death, and what significance did he attach to it? The same consideration holds good for the proclamation of the resurrection; it

always refers back from itself. The risen and exalted Christ, whom the apostles preached and to whom the Christian community prayed, has features–lineaments and traits of personality–with which the disciples were familiar, the lineaments and traits of their earthly lord. The same is true of Paul and all the rest of the preaching of the early church: they also constantly point back behind themselves. Paul fought the self-righteousness of Jewish legalism, the self-complacency of the pious and their self-glorification, against which he set the message that we are saved by faith alone, that God offers salvation, not to the righteous, but to the sinner who trusts alone in His forgiveness. But just that, although couched in other terms, is the very message of Jesus. It is clear that we cannot understand the message of Paul unless we know the message of Jesus. Whatever statements of the kerygma we may care to examine, their origins are always to be found in the message of Jesus. That the primitive church was clearly aware of this is shown by the fact that it supplemented the kerygma (the missionary preaching) with the didache (instruction for the community),[18] which is reflected not only in the epistles and the book of Revelation but also in the gospels. At no time was there a kerygma in the primitive church without didache.

This, then, is the first consideration: we *must* continually return to the historical Jesus and his message. The sources demand it; the kerygma, which refers us back from itself, also demands it. To put it in theological terms, the Incarnation implies that the story of Jesus is not only a possible subject for historical research, study, and criticism, but demands all of

18 ["Didache," a Greek term transliterated into English, means literally "teaching." It has been employed by C. H. Dodd and many others to refer to the teaching activity, especially ethical in its content, which followed after the kerygma among converts in the early church. While many scholars tend to limit the didache to ethical instruction alone, Professor Jeremias views it as reiterating and expanding the kerygma about Jesus' death and as covering all areas of Christian instruction, not just morals; cf. J. Jeremias, *The Sermon on the Mount* (trans. Norman Perrin; "Facet Books, Biblical Series," 2; Philadelphia: Fortress, 1963), pp. 19-21, or R. H. Mounce, *The Essential Nature of New Testament Preaching* (Grand Rapids: Eerdmans, 1960), pp. 40-43, 133.—EDITOR.]

these. We need to know who the Jesus of history was, and what was the content of his message. We may not avoid the offense of the Incarnation. And if it is objected that we fail to apprehend the essential nature of faith if we make historical knowledge the object of faith, and that faith is in this way offered up to such dubious, subjective, and hypothetical study, we can only reply that God has offered up himself. The Incarnation is the self-offering of God, and to that we can only bow in assent.

Indeed, it is precisely at this point that the latest theological developments push on beyond Bultmann's theology of the kerygma. It is now generally acknowledged that the problem of the historical Jesus must be taken seriously, and thus the situation in present-day New Testament studies is not so heterogeneous as it might seem at first sight.

Bulwarks Against the Modernizing of Jesus

We must venture forth on the road to the historical Jesus and his message, no matter where it may lead us. But, and this is the second consideration, we *can* venture on it with confidence, nor need we fear that we are engaging in a perilous, fruitless adventure. The question arises, however, whether we may not be in danger of ending up once again with a subjective, modernized life of Jesus. Is there not a risk that we too, like the whole of the nineteenth century, unconsciously and unintentionally, may project our own theology back into Jesus of Nazareth? With regard to this risk, it must be said that it is certainly never wholly possible for the historian to divest himself of his own personality. We shall never be entirely able to exclude this source of danger. Nevertheless we need not give up in despair, for our position is entirely different from that of the previous century. We are in fact better equipped. Our aims have become more modest, because the mistakes of the "classical" quest of the historical Jesus serve as warnings to us not to want to know more than we can know; that is already a point of inestimable worth. The decisive point, however, is that we today possess, if I may use a metaphor, bulwarks which will protect us from arbitrary modernizations of Jesus, that is, which will protect us from ourselves.

Here I may content myself with suggestions and briefly indicate five aspects of the case.

(1) The critical scholarship of the previous century has thrown up the first bulwark for us in the shape of the remarkable literary criticism which it developed and increasingly refined. We have been taught to distinguish sources or, more correctly (since we are becoming more and more skeptical about the assumption of written sources), strands of tradition: a Marcan tradition, a Logia tradition,[19] the special traditions of Luke, Matthew, and John. Having established this, literary criticism leads us back to the stage of oral tradition antedating our gospels. We have, moreover, been taught to recognize the style of composition of the evangelists, and hence to distinguish between tradition and redaction. We have been thus enabled to trace the tradition back into its pre-literary stage.

(2) Form criticism has led us a step further back by attempting to determine the laws which governed the shaping of the material; it has thus thrown light from another side upon the creation and growth of the tradition. It is a fact not sufficiently known or heeded that the essential significance of form criticism is that it has enabled us to remove a Hellenistic layer which had overlaid an earlier Palestinian tradition.

(3) We have been carried an important step further on the way back to Jesus himself by studies about the world of his day which have disclosed to us his environment, informing us of the religious climate and of Palestinian customs in his day. I am referring to the study of rabbinical literature and of Late

[19] ["Logia," the Greek term for "sayings," is applied to the collection of sayings commonly called "Q" which Matthew and Luke used as a source in addition to their Marcan source. While "Q" is often thought to have been a written book, Professor Jeremias prefers to think of it as an oral stratum of tradition.—EDITOR.]

Jewish apocalyptic. As one who was privileged to live in Palestine for some years, I can testify from my own experience how much new light has been thrown in this way upon the gospels. The importance of the study of both ancient and modern Palestine does not lie primarily in the fact that it has revealed to us how Jesus belonged to his own time; its main significance lies rather in the way in which it has helped us to realize afresh the sharpness of Jesus' opposition to the religiosity of his time. And this is the chief significance of the Dead Sea Scrolls for New Testament studies. The Essenism which they disclose to us enables us to realize from their own testimony to what an extent the whole of Late Judaism was imbued with a passion to establish God's holy community. We can now assess more clearly than heretofore the significance of the emphatic denial with which Jesus met all these attempts.

(4) A further result of the study of the environment of Jesus has been to force upon us the necessity of studying his mother tongue. It was some seventy years ago that Dalman proved conclusively, in my estimation, that Jesus spoke Galilean Aramaic.[20] Since then the study of this dialect has been pursued but is still only in an early stage. We still lack critical editions of the texts and a vocabulary of Galilean Aramaic. But the studies made so far have already demonstrated how rewarding such meticulous philological research can be. It is only necessary to recall in how many cases one and the same saying of Jesus has been transmitted to us in different Greek forms.[21] In most of these cases we are dealing with translation variants, which constitute a reliable aid in reconstructing the Aramaic form of the saying underlying the

[20] [Gustav Dalman, *Die Worte Jesu mit Berücksichtigung des nachkanonischen jüdischen Schrifttums und der aramäischen Sprache erörtert* (Leipzig: J. C. Hinrichs'sche Buchhandlung, 1898; [2]1930); Eng. trans. by D. M. Kay, *The Words of Jesus considered in the light of post-Biblical Jewish writings and the Aramaic language* (Edinburgh: T. & T. Clark, 1902).—EDITOR.]

[21] [On "translation variants," cf. J. Jeremias, *The Sermon on the Mount*, *op. cit.*, pp. 15-16.—EDITOR.]

various versions. For example, the Lord's Prayer, the Greek renderings of which in Matthew and Luke show many divergences, can by this means be retranslated into Jesus' mother tongue with a high degree of probability.[22] Anyone who has ever had anything to do with translations is aware that they can never take the place of the original, and will be able to assess how important it is that we should be able to get back with a high degree of probability to the original Aramaic underlying the Greek tradition. It must of course be remembered that the earliest Christian community spoke Aramaic too; so not every Aramaism is evidence of authenticity. At any rate, however, we are drawing nearer to Jesus himself when we succeed in rediscovering the pre-Hellenistic form of the tradition. In this connection it is of special importance to note that this kind of study reveals peculiarities in the utterances of Jesus which are without contemporary parallels. As a form of address to God the word *abba* is without parallel in the whole of Late Jewish devotional literature.[23] Similarly there is no contemporary analogy to Jesus' use of "Amen" as an introduction to his own utterances.[24] It may be maintained that these two characteristic features of the *ipsissima vox* of Jesus[25] contain in a nutshell his message and his consciousness of his authority.

(5) Of special significance as a bulwark against a psycho-

[22] [Cf. J. Jeremias, *The Lord's Prayer* ("Facet Books, Biblical Series," 8; Philadelphia: Fortress Press, 1964), p. 15.—EDITOR.]

[23] [*Ibid.*, p. 19; cf. also his *Central Message of the New Testament,* pp. 9-30.—EDITOR.]

[24] [H. Schlier, *"amēn,"* in *Theologisches Wörterbuch zum Neuen Testament,* (ed. G. Kittel), Vol. 1 (Stuttgart: W. Kohlhammer, 1933), pp. 339-42, especially 341-42; Eng. trans. by G. W. Bromiley, *Theological Dictionary of the New Testament,* Vol. 1 (Grand Rapids: Eerdmans, 1964), pp. 335-38. While Schlier speaks of Jesus' use of "Amen" as containing "the whole of Christology in nuce," he does not stress the uniqueness of Jesus' usage or draw out the implications as sharply as Professor Jeremias has.—EDITOR.]

[25] [*Ipsissima vox,* Jesus' own original way of speaking. Cf. J. Jeremias, "Characteristics of the ipsissima vox Jesu," in *The Prayers of Jesus* ("Studies in Biblical Theology, second series," 6; London: SCM, 1967).—EDITOR.]

logical modernizing of Jesus is the rediscovery of the eschatological character of his message. It is not only that we have learned to recognize how extensively Jesus shared the conceptions of contemporary apocalyptic and made use of its language; the decisive importance of this discovery lies elsewhere. We have seen how the whole message of Jesus flowed from an awareness that God was about to break into history, an awareness of the approaching crisis, the coming judgment; and we have seen the significance of the fact that it was against this background that he proclaimed the present in-breaking in his own ministry of the kingdom of God.[26]

It is clear, then, that Jesus was no Jewish rabbi, no teacher of wisdom, no prophet, but that his proclamation of a God who was at the present moment offering a share in salvation to the despised, the oppressed, and the despairing ran counter to all the religiosity of his time, and was in truth the end of Judaism.

At the end of his book *The Quest of the Historical Jesus*, Albert Schweitzer has summed up graphically the outcome of the attempts to write a life of Jesus: "The study of the Life of Jesus has had a curious history. It set out in quest of the historical Jesus, believing that when it had found Him it could bring Him straight into our time as a Teacher and Saviour. It loosed the bands by which He had been riveted for centuries to the stony rocks of ecclesiastical doctrine, and rejoiced to see life and movement coming into the figure once more, and the historical Jesus advancing, as it seemed, to meet it. But He does not stay; He passes by our time and returns to His own."[27] Such was in fact the remarkable outcome of the study of the life of Jesus begun in 1778. It had freed Jesus from fetters; he became a living figure, belonging to the present; he became a man of our own time. Yet he did not stay, but passed by our time and returned to his own. It became clear that he was not a man of our time, but the prophet of Nazareth, who spoke the language of the prophets of the old covenant and

26 [Cf. J. Jeremias, *The Parables of Jesus*, *op. cit.*—Editor.]

27 *Op. cit.*, Eng. trans., p. 397.

proclaimed the God of the old covenant. But we must now extend Schweitzer's metaphor. Jesus did not stay in his own time, but he also passed beyond his own time. He did not remain the rabbi of Nazareth, the prophet of Late Judaism. He receded into the distance, entered into the dim light of Easter morning, and became, as Schweitzer says in the closing sentence of his book, the One unknown, without a name, who speaks the word, "Follow thou me!"[28]

Historical Study and Jesus' Claim

If we travel the road thus indicated, threading our way amid the five protecting walls which guard us from modernizing Jesus and fashioning him in our own likeness, we are then confronted by a unique claim to authority which breaks through the bounds of the Old Testamant and of Judaism. Everywhere we are confronted in the message of Jesus by this ultimate claim, that is to say, we are confronted by the same claim to faith as that with which the kerygma presents us. We must at this point reiterate one of the simplest and most obvious facts, since it is no longer obvious to all. Every sentence of the sources bears witness of this fact to us, every verse of our gospels hammers it into us: something has happened, something unique, something which had never happened before. The study of the history of religions has amassed countless parallels and analogies to the message of Jesus. As far as our knowledge of Pharisaic and rabbinical theology is concerned, for instance, the monumental work of Paul Billerbeck[29] is unsurpassed and will long remain so. Yet the more analogies we amass, the clearer it becomes that there are no analogies to the message of Jesus. There is no

[28] *Ibid.*, p. 401.

[29] [H. Strack and P. Billerbeck, *Kommentar zum Neuen Testament aus Talmud und Midrasch* (6 vols.; Munich: C. H. Beck, 1922-61). The four volumes of commentary from Jewish sources were published between 1922 and 1928 and are exclusively the work of Paul Billerbeck. Volume 4 actually consists of two parts, containing detached notes on various important topics. Vols. 5 and 6 add valuable indices prepared under Professor Jeremias' direction.—Editor.]

parallel to his message that God is concerned with sinners and not with the righteous, and that he grants them, here and now, a share in his kingdom. There is no parallel to Jesus' sitting down in table-fellowship with publicans and sinners. There is no parallel to the authority with which he dares to address God as *abba*. Anyone who admits merely the fact—and I cannot see how it can be gainsaid—that the word *abba* is an authentic utterance of Jesus, is, if he understands the word correctly, without watering down its meaning, thereby confronted with Jesus' claim to authority. Anyone who reads the parable of the Prodigal Son, which belongs to the bedrock of the tradition, and observes how in this parable, which describes the unimaginable goodness of divine forgiveness, Jesus justifies his table-fellowship with publicans and sinners, is again confronted with the claim of Jesus to be regarded as God's representative, acting with his authority.[30] One example after another could be cited, but the result would always be the same. If with utmost discipline and conscientiousness we apply the critical resources at our disposal to the study of the historical Jesus, the final result is always the same: we find ourselves confronted with God himself. That is the fact to which the sources bear witness: a man appeared, and those who received his message were certain that they had heard the word of God. It is not as if faith were made superfluous or belittled, when exegesis shows us that behind every word and every deed of Jesus lies his claim to authority. (How could faith ever become superfluous?) Indeed, the truth of the matter is that through the words and acts of Jesus at every turn the challenge to faith is presented. When we read the gospels, even when we read them critically, we cannot evade this challenge. This claim to divine authority is the origin of Christianity, and hence study of the historical Jesus and his message is no peripheral task of New Testament scholarship, a study of one particular historical problem among many others. It is *the* central task of New Testament scholarship.

[30] Cf. E. Fuchs, "Die Frage nach dem historischen Jesus," *op. cit.*, p. 219 (Eng. trans., pp. 20-21). [Cf. also J. Jeremias, *The Parables of Jesus, op. cit.*, pp. 128-32 in the rev. ed.—EDITOR.]

3

THE GOOD NEWS OF JESUS AND THE PROCLAMATION OF THE EARLY CHURCH

THIS brings us to one final query. If it is true that the good news of Jesus in word and deed is the origin of Christianity, then it may be asked: What is the relation between the good news of Jesus and the early church's witness of faith? What is the relation between the pre-resurrection and the post-resurrection message, between the gospel and the kerygma? With regard to these questions there are two things to be said.

(1) The good news of Jesus and the early church's witness of faith are inseparable from one another. Neither of these may be treated in isolation. For the gospel of Jesus remains dead history without the witness of faith by the church, which continually reiterates, affirms, and attests this gospel afresh. Nor can the kerygma be treated in isolation either. Apart from Jesus and his gospel the kerygma is merely the proclamation of an idea or a theory. To isolate the message of Jesus leads to Ebionitism; to isolate the kerygma of the early church leads to Docetism.[31]

[31] [Ebionitism was the variety of Jewish Christianity which separated from the church and became a sect emphasizing the necessity of the Law for salvation; it opposed Paul and presented only a minimal Christology, seeing in Jesus only a man filled by the Spirit of God. For "Docetism," cf. note 17, above. Ebionitism severed its connection with the church of which Paul was an apostle; Docetism contested the connection of faith with the story of Jesus in all its stark reality.—EDITOR.]

(2) If, then, these two belong together, the gospel of Jesus and the early church's witness of faith, and if neither of these may be isolated, it is also of utmost importance to recognize—and this is decisive—that they are not both on the same level. The gospel of Jesus and the kerygma of the early church must not be placed on the same footing, but they are related to one another as call and response. The life, acts, and death of Jesus, the authoritative word of him who dared to say *abba*, the one who with divine authority invited sinners to his table, and as the servant of God went to the cross—all this is the call of God. The early church's witness of faith, the Spirit-led chorus of a thousand tongues, is the response to God's call. The ancient church liked to express this relationship in pictorial representations of the cosmic liturgy, in the midst of which is depicted a gigantic figure of the Crucified, toward whom, from the right and the left, there streams a countless throng on earth and in heaven. What such representations say is that Jesus of Nazareth is God's call to his creatures; confession of him is their response. This response always has a double aspect: it is praise and adoration of God, and witness to the world. It is inspired by the Spirit of God, but it does not take the place of the call. The call, not the response, is the decisive thing. The many-sided witness of the early church—of Paul, of John, of the Epistle to the Hebrews—must be judged in light of the message of Jesus.

Underlying our protest against the equating of the gospel and the kerygma is a concern for the concept of revelation. According to the witness of the New Testament, there is no other revelation of God but the incarnate Word. The preaching of the early church, on the other hand, is the divinely inspired witness *to* the revelation, but the church's preaching is not itself the revelation. To put it bluntly, revelation does not take place from eleven to twelve o'clock on Sunday morning. Golgotha is not everywhere; there is only *one* Golgotha, and it lies just outside the walls of Jerusalem.[32]

[32] P. Althaus, *Das sogenannte Kerygma, op. cit.*, p. 34; Eng. trans., p. 58.

The doctrine of continuous revelation *(revelatio continua)* is a gnostic heresy. No, the church's proclamation is, from its earliest beginnings, not itself revelation, but it does guide toward the Revelation. This, at any rate, is the way Paul conceived of the task of the kerygma when he told the Galatians that the content of his preaching had been the depiction of Christ crucified before their eyes. (Gal. 3:1; cf. I Cor. 2:2).

Once more: according to the witness of the New Testament, the church's proclamation is not revelation, but it leads to the revelation. Jesus is the Lord. The Lord is above the one who proclaims the message. For faith, there is no other authority but the Lord. Hence, the historical Jesus and his message are not *one* presupposition among many for the kerygma, but the *sole* presupposition of the kerygma. Thus, indeed, the response presupposes the call, and the witness to the revelation presupposes the revelation. Only the Son of man and his word can give authority to the proclamation. No one else and nothing else.

For Further Reading

BY JOACHIM JEREMIAS:

The Parables of Jesus. London: SCM, and New York: Scribner's, 1954; rev. ed., 1963. Condensed version, *Rediscovering the Parables.* London: SCM (paperback), 1966, and New York: Scribner's, 1967.

The Eucharistic Words of Jesus. Oxford: Basil Blackwell, and New York: Macmillan, 1955. Rev. ed., London: SCM (paperback), and New York: Scribner's, 1966.

Unknown Sayings of Jesus. London: SPCK, and Greenwich, Conn.: Seabury, 1957; rev. ed., 1964.

The Servant of God (written with WALTHER ZIMMERLI). ("Studies in Biblical Theology," 20.) London: SCM, and Naperville: Allenson, 1957; rev. ed., 1965.

Jesus' Promise to the Nations. ("Studies in Biblical Theology," 24.) London: SCM, and Naperville: Allenson, 1958.

The Origins of Infant Baptism: A further study in reply to Kurt Aland. ("Studies in Historical Theology," 1.) London: SCM, and Naperville: Allenson, 1963.

The Central Message of the New Testament. London: SCM, and New York: Scribner's, 1965.

Jerusalem in the Time of Jesus. Philadelphia: Fortress, 1969.

The Prayers of Jesus. ("Studies in Biblical Theology, Second Series," 6.) London: SCM, and Naperville: Allenson, 1967. (A selection from the volume of collected essays, *Abba: Studien zur neutestamentliche Theologie und Zeitgeschichte* [Göttingen: Vandenhoeck & Ruprecht, 1966].)

New Testament Theology Volume I: The Proclamation of Jesus. New York: Scribner's, 1971.

On the Problem of the Historical Jesus
(in the order in which titles are referred to in the introduction):

Professor Jeremias' own bibliography of the most important works is given on p. 1, n. 1.

GRANT, ROBERT M. *The Earliest Lives of Jesus.* London: SPCK, and New York: Harper, 1961.

MCARTHUR, HARVEY K. *The Quest Through the Centuries: The Search for the Historical Jesus.* Philadelphia: Fortress, 1966.

MITCHELL, E. K. "History of the Life of Christ," in *Recent Christian Progress.* New York: Macmillan, 1909. Pp. 118–26. Covers seventy-five years prior to 1909.

CASE, SHIRLEY JACKSON. "The Life of Jesus during the Last Quarter-Century," *The Journal of Religion,* 5 (1925), 561–75. Covers 1900–1925.

——*Jesus through the Centuries.* University of Chicago Press, 1932.

For Further Reading

HUNTER, A. M. "The Life of Christ in the Twentieth Century," *The Expository Times,* 61 (1950), 131-35. Reprinted in *Interpreting the New Testament 1900–1950* (Philadelphia: Westminster, 1951), pp. 49–60.

ROWLINGSON, D. T. "The Continuing Quest of the Historical Jesus," in *New Testament Studies: Critical Essays in New Testament Interpretation with Special Reference to the Meaning and Worth of Jesus,* ed. E. P. BOOTH. New York: Abingdon-Cokesbury, 1942. Pp. 42–69. Covers 1918 to 1942.

KÜMMEL, W. G. "Jesusforschung seit 1950," *Theologische Rundschau,* Neue Folge, 31 (1966), 15–46, 289–315.

PERRIN, NORMAN. *Rediscovering the Teaching of Jesus.* New York: Harper, 1967. Annotated bibliography, pp. 249–66, covers "the Historical Jesus" and various aspects of his teaching, by the translator of the present essay.

RISTOW, HELMUT, and MATTHIAE, KARL (eds.). *Der historische Jesus und der kerygmatische Christus: Beiträge zum Christusverständnis in Forschung und Verkündigung.* Berlin: Evangelische Verlagsanstalt, 1962. Forty-eight essays in German on the "historical Jesus" and "kerygmatic Christ," by Protestant, Catholic, and Jewish scholars including New Testament experts like Bornkamm, Kümmel, Stauffer, Riesenfeld, Bultmann, and Cullmann, and systematicians like Brunner and Diem. While most of the authors are German, others are Scandinavian, British, and American. Many contributions were originally presented as lectures or published elsewhere. Thirty-six plates depicting Christ in art through the centuries are appended.

SCHUBERT, KURT (ed.). *Der historische Jesus und der Christus unseres Glaubens: Eine Katholische Auseinandersetzung mit der Folgen der Entmythologisierungtheorie.* Vienna and Freiburg: Herder, 1962. A series of essays wherein Roman Catholic biblical scholars on the continent deal with aspects of the "demythologization" discussion, especially with reference to the life of Jesus.

BRAATEN, CARL E., and HARRISVILLE, ROY A. (eds.). *Kerygma and History: A Symposium on the Theology of Rudolf Bultmann.* New York: Abingdon, 1962. Nine essays on the kerygma and related topics. Those by Dahl and Diem are especially pertinent to discussion of the historical Jesus.

BRAATEN, CARL E., and HARRISVILLE, ROY A. (eds.). *The Historical Jesus and the Kerygmatic Christ: Essays on the New Quest of the Historical Jesus.* New York: Abingdon, 1964. Nine essays reflecting current discussion, including Bultmann's famous appraisal of the New Quest in 1959.

The Journal of Bible and Religion, 30, 2 (July, 1962), 198–223. Prints papers by James M. Robinson, Schubert Ogden, and Morton Enslin, read at a symposium on the New Quest in 1961.

Interpretation, 16, 2 (April, 1962), 131–92. Presents five articles on various aspects of the New Quest; that by Bo Reicke particularly deals with the relation of the "historical Jesus" and the "kerygmatic Christ."

FULLER, REGINALD H. *The New Testament in Current Study*. New York: Scribner's, 1962. Pp. 25–53 especially.

ZAHRNT, HEINZ. *The Historical Jesus*. Trans. J. S. BOWDEN. New York: Harper, 1963.

ANDERSON, HUGH. *Jesus and Christian Origins: A Commentary on Modern Viewpoints*. New York: Oxford University Press, 1964.

BULTMANN, RUDOLF. *Jesus and The Word*. Trans. LOUISE PETTIBONE SMITH and ERMINIE HUNTRESS. New York: Scribner's, 1934. Paperback ed., 1958.

BORNKAMM, GUNTHER. *Jesus of Nazareth*. Trans. IRENE and FRASER MCLUSKEY with JAMES M. ROBINSON. New York: Harper, 1960.

ENSLIN, MORTON S. *The Prophet from Nazareth*. New York: McGraw-Hill, 1961.

STAUFFER, ETHELBERT. *Jesus and His Story*. Trans. RICHARD and CLARA WINSTON, New York: Knopf, 1959; or trans. DOROTHEA M. BARTON, London: SCM, 1960.

MCCASLAND, S. VERNON. *The Pioneer of Our Faith: A New Life of Jesus*. New York: McGraw-Hill, 1964.

GLOEGE, GERHARD. *The Day of His Coming: The Man in the Gospels*. Trans. STANLEY RUDMAN. Philadelphia: Fortress, 1963.

GOGUEL, MAURICE. *Jesus and the Origins of Christianity*. Trans. OLIVE WYON. New York: Macmillan, 1933. Paperback ed., New York: Harper, 1960.

MANSON, T. W. "The Quest of the Historical Jesus—Continued," in *Studies in the Gospels and Epistles*, ed. MATTHEW BLACK. Philadelphia: Westminster, 1962. Pp. 3–12; cf. 13–145 also.

BROWN, RAYMOND E., S.S. "After Bultmann, What?—An Introduction to the Post-Bultmannians," *Catholic Biblical Quarterly*, 26 (1964), 1–30.

CAHILL, P. JOSEPH, S.J. "Rudolf Bultmann and Post-Bultmannian Tendencies," *Catholic Biblical Quarterly*, 26 (1964), 153–78. Reprinted in *New Theology No. 2*, ed. M. E. MARTY and D. G. PEERMAN (New York: Macmillan, 1965), 222–54.

KÄSEMANN, ERNST. "Blind Alleys in the 'Jesus of History' Controversy," in *New Testament Questions of Today*. Trans. W. J. MONTAGUE. Philadelphia: Fortress, 1969. Pp. 23 65.

Facet Books Available

Biblical Series:

1. *The Significance of the Bible for the Church*
   by Anders Nygren (translated by Carl Rasmussen). 1963
2. *The Sermon on the Mount*
   by Joachim Jeremias (translated by Norman Perrin). 1963
5. *The Meaning of Hope*
   by C. F. D. Moule. 1963
7. *The Genesis Accounts of Creation*
   by Claus Westermann (translated by Norman E. Wagner). 1964
8. *The Lord's Prayer*
   by Joachim Jeremias (translated by John Reumann). 1964
9. *Only to the House of Israel? Jesus and the Non-Jews*
   by T. W. Manson. 1964
13. *The Problem of the Historical Jesus*
   by Joachim Jeremias (translated by Norman Perrin). 1964
15. *The Bible and the Role of Women*
   by Krister Stendahl (translated by Emilie T. Sander). 1966
19. *The Psalms: A Form-Critical Introduction*
   by Hermann Gunkel (translated by Thomas M. Horner). 1967
20. *The Spirit-Paraclete in the Fourth Gospel*
   by Hans Windisch (translated by James W. Cox). 1968
25. *The Lord's Supper as a Christological Problem*
   by Willi Marxsen (translated by Lorenz Nieting). 1970
26. *The "I Am" of the Fourth Gospel*
   by Philip B. Harner. 1970
27. *The Gospels and Contemporary Biographies in the Greco-Roman World*
   by Clyde Weber Votaw. 1970
28. *Was Jesus a Revolutionist?*
   by Martin Hengel (translated by William Klassen). 1971
29. *Iscariot*
   by Bertil Gärtner (translated by Victor I. Gruhn). 1971
30. *Eschatology in Luke*
   by E. Earle Ellis. 1972
31. *Beginning and End in the Bible*
   by Claus Westermann (translated by Keith Crim). 1972

27. *The Gospels and Contemporary Biographies in the Greco-Roman World*
   by Clyde Weber Votaw. 1970
28. *Was Jesus a Revolutionist?*
   by Martin Hengel (translated by William Klassen). 1971
29. *Iscariot*
   by Bertil Gartner (translated by Victor I. Gruhn). 1971
30. *Eschatology in Luke*
   by E. Earle Ellis. 1972
31. *Beginning and End in the Bible*
   by Claus Westermann (translated by Keith Crim). 1972